OFFICE 365

USER GUIDE

D1413429

DATE DUE

CONTENTS

INTRODUCTION

Office 365 is one of the fastest-growing products in Microsoft's history. People are using Office 365 as they upgrade from the traditional Microsoft Office which can be purchased in a store install. With Microsoft Office 365, now you can sign up for, subscribe and download an Office 365 subscription and download and install Office products to your devices. Oh, and you don't have to worry about upgrading because as a subscription-based product you are always guaranteed to have the latest apps and updates as Microsoft releases them. Organizations large and small have been moving their infrastructure over to the Microsoft cloud and are reaping the cost savings, predictability, and peace of mind that comes with the cloud. Because Microsoft has included almost all of their popular Enterprise products in the Office 365 offering, it becomes a game-changer from the very beginning. As with any technology, however, there is a learning curve. Microsoft has done everything they could to make Office 365 as user friendly and intuitive as possible

In the last decade, the cloud has taken the information technology community by storm. As companies have struggled with the learning curve and cost of adopting Enterprise-class software on their own the cloud has created a simplified and streamlined alternative. The complexity of keeping software running has been taken out of the equation. The result is that organizations can focus on using software to drive business and competitive advantage instead of using critical resources to keep the lights blinking green.

Office 365 is the cloud offering by Microsoft and bundles popular server software such as SharePoint, Exchange, and

Skype for Business, along with such consumer software as Office Word, Excel, PowerPoint, OneNote, and Outlook into a single product that is accessed over the Internet and paid for on a monthly basis per user. The consumer products are downloadable to many different devices, including iPhones, iPads, Macs, and Android-based phones and tablets, in addition to the familiar Windows-based devices. Microsoft runs the server products in their data centers with their engineers; you can be assured that they know what they are doing. After all, who is better off managing these products than the same people who actually built them in the first place? To ease the mind of the risk-averse, Microsoft puts their company name and piles of cash behind Office 365 in a very attractive service level agreement. For those who are still not convinced the cloud is the place to be, Microsoft has taken the unique step of designing Office 365 in a way that lets you use Office 365 for your enterprise in a hybrid environment. Should you want to keep some of your data and management in-house you can still use Office 365. If you feel more comfortable moving to Office 365 in waves, then it is designed to accommodate you. You can start with a pilot group in order to prove the benefits that the cloud provides before turning your trust over to Microsoft engineers. Microsoft is convinced that after you try Office 365, it will change your perspective on Enterprise software forever, and you will never look back.

CHAPTER ONE
WANT TO SIGN UP FOR OFFICE 365?

Signing up for Microsoft office 365 can be achieved free of charge and within a very short time. It takes only a few minutes and you won't need to use a credit card or other purchasing tool as it's totally free. When using the free trial pack which usually lasts for 30 days allows you to share your trial with as many as 25 users.

TIPS FOR EASY SIGNING UP TO OFFICE 365

If you want to sign up for the trial, always remember to follow this important procedure:

a) Carefully choose an organization name. You will continue to use the name of the organization you choose beyond the trial period. It is relevant for your final deployment plans.

b) Choose an organizational name that is simple which your trial users will recognize and remember easily. For instance, if the name of your organization is Jonajones, this is how the name would be used in your URLs:

❖ Sign-in credentials and email address: user@jonajones.onmicrosoft.com
❖ Team site: http://jonajones.sharepoint.com
❖ Newsfeed: http://jonajones-my.sharepoint.com

After you have done signing up successfully, you will be logged into your trial as the first admin.

Always remember to come back to Office 365 Fast Track to continue setting up your trial.

At this level, you are ready to sign up for a free trial of Office 365.

HOW DO YOU SET UP YOUR INITIAL DOMAIN?

There is a reward you get for signing up for Office 365, have you experienced the rigor in getting a domain name to purchase from web designers and IT professionals? Well! You will receive a free default domain (your Microsoft.com domain) If you know the price for getting a domain or ever experience the stress, then you would understand the value of the reward you get when you sign up for Office 365, and even if you have not, the good news is that as part of your signing up for Office 365, you receive a default domain free, which you can use to do some things effectively without having to change anything on your existing DNS records. Here is how to configure your onmicrosoft.com domain:

❖ In the Office 365 admin center, **click setup.**
❖ In the quick start, section click **start.**
❖ On the **Choose a domain** page, select the onmicrosoft.com domain.
❖ Click **Next** to come.

WANT TO ADD USERS TO THE TRIAL?

All the trial users can be added at this point. You can start by adding a few users then continue subsequently. Many organizations would usually open the domain environment and give access to their IT and help desk staff first, then to key business users afterward. Usually, when those IT and Help Desk staff who are given access first would help to support other users. If are going to use this process involving two–steps, then you have will consider creating all the trial accounts first, and provide the sign–in information for the remaining users when you are ready for each group to join your office 365 domain or environment.

Should you prefer to add one user at a time, then you'd have to follow these simple guidelines to **create or edit users in Office 365**. This is the fastest way to add a small group of people to your environment without having to waste much time.

To add a lot of people to your domain at once, follow the steps **add multiple users with a CVS file** or **you use Windows PowerShell cmdlets for Office 365.**

WANT TO TRY OUTLOOK WEB ACCESS?

 For the users to what the Outlook Web Access experience is like, they should use the connected accounts to send and receive email messages from their existing mailboxes without having to move any email. The connected account featured downloads a copy of the current inbox email for immediate use in their Office 365 mailbox. This also allows users to send and receive email from an existing email address without the hassle of disrupting mail routing.

Are you having an already configured POP3 or IMAP4 access to the mailbox in your organization? Then, there is only one required preparation for you to do, and that is to validate that you can add a connected account to your administrator mailbox. But if you have not enabled these protocols for your organization, there is no course for alarm. All you need to do is enable the protocols before validating that you can add connected accounts to the administrator mailbox.

WANT TO TRY A SHAREPOINT COLLABORATION SITE?

Once you sign up for Office 365, a good number of site collections are automatically created for you. During your trial, we recommend that you create a new private site collection to test team collaboration with your users. A new site collection will provide you the freedom to experiment, and if you choose to delete it at the end of your trial, you will not run into any of the problems that might likely occur if you delete the original private site collection that is created for you when you signed up.

COLLABORATING MADE EASY

In the last decade, SharePoint has taken the world by storm. A consultant friend of mine once shared an experience he had in a conference that he facilitated at the Transcorp Hilton Hotel in Abuja, Nigeria. After his lecture, he gave room for Questions and Answers and a large property management client asked about SharePoint. Somehow, my friend was curious and was wondering what informed the participant's question, as his topic of discussion was unrelated to the question he raised, and at the same time, he didn't want to leave the fellow unattended. My friend narrated "this man told me that when he talks with his peers in the industry, they all tell him they use SharePoint extensively. When he asks them about their experience using SharePoint they tell him that they can't imagine running their business without SharePoint. That was enough of a driver for him to find out about SharePoint right away. After all, when the competition moves toward something that increases their advantage, other companies have to move quickly in order to maintain the ability to compete. And this is the case with the adoption of the technology wave consisting of communication, collaboration, content management, and consolidation, which is all made possible by SharePoint.

With Office 365, your organization gets SharePoint without the hassle of having to work through a complicated deployment. Your IT staff has an administrative interface and can get provision sites and set up users with minimal effort. With SharePoint up and running, your organization can spend its resources on solving real business problems with SharePoint, instead of working through the technical details of implementation.

PREPARING THE USERS FOR THE TRIAL

There is an email template that Microsoft provides which you can easily use to notify your users that they will soon be a part of an Office 365 trial. This email contains a welcome message and overview of Office 365. To get the email template from Microsoft:

       a. Download the **Introducing Office 365 template.**

b. Edit the template to add whatever you expect of your users during the trial.

READY TO TEST RUN YOUR OFFICE 365?

At this stage, all your Office 365 services are ready to be tried, but you must take out time to try some of the features yourself first, or with a small set of initial trial users before you add the rest of your users. A test run allows you to have some administrative experience in Office 365, and this will help your users to ramp up on the services. If you would like to test run your Office 365 right away, follow these simple steps:

a. **Message;** send out an email message to each other.
b. **Share docs**; Use OneDrive for Business to share docs with one another or use your first team site
c. **Online Meeting**; the next thing to do is set an online meeting to discuss your plans.

TRY OFFICE 365 WITH YOUR USERS

To do this, you are now ready to roll out your Office 365 to other users. Quickly **download the office 365 pilot template,** then copy the contents into your email message, and the message to the users so they can have the information they will need to get started at:

❖ Office 365 portal: **https://portal.microsoftonline.com**
❖ Outlook Web App: **https://mail.office365.com**

❖ Directions for setting up mobile devices: **Settings ≥ Office 365 settings ≥ Get started ≥ Phone & tablet**

❖ <u>**Office 365 tips and ideas**</u>

❖ Contact information for support staff

CHAPTER TWO
DEPLOYING OFFICE 365 TO ORGANIZATION

Would you like to deploy Office 365 in your organization now?

The deployment of Office 365 in your organization begins with preparing your network and checking for seemingly possible issues to eliminate them. The resources and every tool you would require for that are going to be provided here just follow carefully as we review the requirements and guide you into all you will need along the way.

The setup process for deploying Office 365 in your organization could take less than a day to a few days to complete depending on the complexity of your deployment.

CONVERTING YOUR TRIAL INTO A PAID SUBSCRIPTION

Now is the time to convert into a paid subscription. If you are still, using the trial tenant, quickly follow the instruction to complete the conversion process.

SET UP YOUR OWN DOMAIN

You will need to change from the free automatic default onmicrosoft.com domain, and then add your own domain to Office 365 so that the user's email address will be on your organization's domain.

WONDERING HOW TO ADD DOMAIN?

You can add your own domain seamlessly by following the following steps:

i. Go to the Office 365 admin center and Click **Domains,** and then click **Add a domain.** Adding users can be skipped for now

ii. Create a record at your DNS hosting provider or domain registrar to verify that you are the owner of the domain.

iii. State the purpose for the domain by defining how you would use the domain or what it would be used for. To do that, select the Office 365 services you are planning to use: Exchange Online, Lync Online, SharePoint Online, or a combination of those services.

iv. Update your DNS records at your hosting provider or domain registrar to point to these services in Office 365.

UPDATE YOUR DEFAULT DOMAIN

There is one important task to complete after you have verified your domain. That is to change your free automatic Microsoft default domain from onmicrosoft.com to the custom domain you just added.

Click your organization's name in the upper–right corner in the Office 365 admin center, and then select the **default domain.**

TRANSFERRING YOUR TRIAL USERS TO YOUR DOMAIN

You have to move your trial users and existing email to the environment or the domain that you just added, because that your deployment is your own domain now.

NOTIFY YOUR EXISTING TRIAL USERS

Call or send a message to your trial users to inform or notify them of your intended switch before you do it to prepare their mind, let them know that they will be using Office 365 now for your email and collaboration. Ensure to provide them with all the necessary information to help them know what they need to do so that the Outlook, mobile phone, OneDrive for Business, and other Office applications will continue to for them seamlessly.

Mobile Phones Update: It is not hard to update the mobile phone configuration. Once the user ID is changed to Office 365, the mobile phone would prompt the users for new sign–in information. Enter the new user ID and the existing password, and then the user's mobile phone will reconnect to Office 365. If the user doesn't get to receive the prompting alert or message on his or her mobile phone for credentials, he can follow **instructions to set up and use Office 365 on a mobile phone or tablet.**

Outlook: Your trial users who use Outlook would be prompted for their new credentials. What the user needs to do is just type his or her new user ID and existing Office 365 password to continue using the profile. If the user doesn't get the prompting message or alert from Outlook, follow the instruction to **change your email account settings.**

Lync: All trial users who would have created Lync meetings before the change of the domain name will have to reschedule the meetings to enable them to function under the new name, because until those meetings are rescheduled, the participants may receive an error message when they try to join any Lync Online meetings and conferences that are scheduled by the user. Also, if you are already using any of the Lync servers: (Lync server 2013, Lync server 2010, or Office Communications server 2007 R2) as part of your existing on–premises environment, you will have to make additional changes to avoid unnecessary interruptions for your users. You can learn how to configure an existing On–premises Lync server deployment using Office 365; follow the instructions to **change your email account settings**

❖ Do you seek help creating a notification? Simply download the **Introducing Office 365 template.**

HOW TO MOVE YOUR TRIAL USERS TO YOUR CUSTOM DOMAIN

You have to make huge progress already since you now have your own custom domain set up in Office 365, however, you will need to move your trial users to that domain to enable them to sign in and receive an email by using an address on your custom domain without the hassle of going through the free automatic domain. (Onmicrosoft.com domain).

Here are the simple steps to move your trial users to your custom domain seamlessly:

- ❖ Follow the instruction to change your user IDs
- ❖ Click Admin, click Exchange, and then follow the instruction to add a new primary email address for the mailbox.

ACTIVATE YOUR YAMMER ENTERPRISE NETWORK

Manual activation of the Yammer Enterprise is required for you to do from the Office 365 Admin Center. This will enable you to have full control of your enterprise social network by using administrative tools like network configuration, user management, advanced integrations, directory synchronization, etc.

Once you have successfully added your company domain and moved Global Administrators to the domain, then activating your Yammer Enterprise Network can easily be done by following these simple steps:

❖ Go to Office 365 Admin Center, click <u>Dashboard</u>, and then click on <u>Included Services</u>
❖ Click Yes, to activate Yammer Enterprise for my network.
❖ Confirm the domain you want to activate.

The company domain which you added earlier would be displayed. You will have to select a single domain that you'd want to activate for your Yammer Enterprise network if you have multiple domains. Note that your Yammer Enterprise cannot work effectively with your activated onmicrosoft.com domain even if you want to use it for Yammer Enterprise.

❖ Click <u>Activate Yammer Enterprise</u>. You will be prompted to wait while the Yammer network activates.
❖ Log into Your Yammer. You now have access as an Office 365 Global Admin, and that gives you access to the Yammer Admin Center as well to be able to configure and manage your Yammer network.

Once the activation is done successfully, every Global Admin on that domain is granted the Yammer Verified Admin rights, and Yammer licenses are given to all the Office 365 users on your account automatically.

ADDING USERS TO YOUR YAMMER NETWORK

Get the users who don't have an account with Yammer yet to create their account by using their company email address from the same domain. Also, those who are already Admin can add users directly via the Yammer user management tools.

MAKING YAMMER YOUR DEFAULT SOCIAL EXPERIENCE

Once you have complete you're the activation of your Yammer Enterprise network, inform your organization to let know. You can activate the simplified login to Yammer from your Office 365 to enable the users to have easy access to the network.

If need further information on activating Yammer Enterprise, such as multiple domains, eligibility, as well as other frequently asked questions, read the Yammer Activation Guide.

To be able to get the best out of your Yammer, go to the Customer Success Center to check out other relevant additional resources.

INTEGRATE YOUR WINDOWS ACTIVE DIRECTORY USERS

All organization that uses an on-premises Windows Active Directory can easily synchronize or integrate with organization's Office 365 tenant for the automation of all cloud-based administrative tasks and to provide users with a more streamlined sign-in experience. That is good news for you if your organization is already using an on-premises Windows Active Directory.

DIRECTORIES SYNCHRONIZATION

Synchronizing directories allows you to sync your on-premises directory objects such as users, groups, contacts, etc to the cloud to help reduce administrative overhead. Directory synchronization is also referred to as *Directory Sync.*

For further information on Windows Azure Active Directory Sync, you can check out <u>Configure Directory Synchronization</u>

PASSWORD SYNCHRONIZATION

When you use a single username and password with your users to log onto your corporate network and resources, you and all the users would be allowed to log into the Windows Azure Active Directory other services available. Password synchronization is one of the features of Directory Synchronizing tools.

Check out <u>Implement Password Synchronization</u>, to get further instructions on how to deploy password synchronization.

You may be required to provide Windows Active Directory remediation before you can synchronize to Office 365; you can use IdFix to reduce the time involved in troubleshooting Windows Active Directory errors that may be reported by the Directory Synchronization tool. <u>IdFix DirSync Error Remediation Tool</u> is available for a quick Download.

BUILDING YOUR SHARE POINT SITE COLLECTIONS AND GROUPS

Site collections will help your organization to provide needed support for internal projects and collaboration. Also, you can use SharePoint groups to manage permissions across site collections. This implies that you will have to build both your site collections before releasing your Office 365 access to the rest of your organization, and set up your SharePoint groups.

Create custom groups or simply assign users to your existing SharePoint groups that you have already created: Take out time and excuse yourself from some personal engagements to work with and study other relevant departments and stakeholders within your organization to enable you to identify the need of the business to have sites before building the site collections as that will help you know how many site collections you will have to create, the type site to create as well as the ideal site template to use and how to configure the site collections.

Visit manage site collections and global settings in the SharePoint Admin Center   And   SharePoint Online Planning Guide for Office 365 and Midsize,   to get further information on how to get started with this process.

 For more information on how to manage permissions to and SharePoint groups, go to Introduction: Control user access with permission

Once you are prepared to build your sites, with these instructions, you will have access to the needed resources to create site collections one at a time in the SharePoint Online Admin Center, or you can create multiple site collections at once and then apply SharePoint groups to them by using PowerShell cmdlets in the SharePoint Online Management Shell.

HOW TO SET UP DEVICES AND DIAL-IN OPTIONS FOR LYNC ONLINE

You can include Lync Online in your subscription and enable your users can connect to meetings and peer-to-peer sessions.

WANT TO MAKE YOUR DEVICES WORK WITH LYNC ONLINE?

How lync work is that it detects your videos as well as your audio devices such as microphones, headphones, cameras, and speakers automatically. It allows you to change your devices if need be any time. You can improve the quality by changing your settings to ensure high quality. Always remember to check your devices before making a call or before joining any meeting.

Visit Set up Lync Audio and Video Devices, to get further information.

SETTING UP YOUR DIAL-IN CONFERENCING

When dial-in conferencing is set, you will be able to add telephone access to Lync Online meetings users who can't get to their computers; this will enable them to join the conference by dialing in from their phones. For further information, visit Configure dial–in conference.

START USING OFFICE 365 IN YOUR ORGANIZATION

Take some time to adequately prepare your users and help desk with the necessary information and orientation they'd need for a smooth transition before you release Office 365 to the rest of your organization.

WONDERING HOW TO PREPARE YOUR HELP DESK?

Ensure you get your help desk staff to acquire all the relevant resources they would need to enable them to help other users that contact them. These are some resources that you will need to share with them before you allow the rest of your organization access to start using the services:

- ❖ Discover Office 365
- ❖ Training courses Office 365 for businesses

HOW TO PREPARE YOUR USERS TO SIGN IN AND START USING OFFICE 365

Notification Email: send each of your users a notification email message with all the information they'll need to get started on Office 365:

- ❖ Office 365 portal: https://portal.microsoftonline.com

- ❖ Outlook Web App: https://mail.office365.com
- ❖ Directions for setting up mobile devices: Settings ≥ Office365 settings ≥ Get started ≥ Phone & tablet
- ❖ Office 365 tips and ideas: https://fastrack.office.com/GettingStarted
- ❖ Contact information for support staff.

Customize message: Use a customized email message for the rest of your users by downloading the Office 365 template here, and sending the necessary information to the users.

By doing these, you would have completed the deployment of Office 365 to your organization successfully.

CHAPTER THREE

OFFICE 365 OPTIONAL CONFIGURATION SETTINGS

Now that you have successfully signed into Office 365 and deployed it to your organization and it's operational for everyone. This part deals with what you will need to do to maximize your Office 365 experience and get it to deliver some more value for you and your organization to enjoy.

DELIVERY OF FEDERATED IDENTITY MANAGEMENT EXPERIENCE

Identity management can be done by activating a single sign-on. When you do it, the users in your organization would be enabled to have access to Office 365 services with fewer prompts. This will also allow you to enact your organization's account restrictions and password policies.

Visit: prepare for directory synchronization, for further information about identity management.

CREATE UNIFIED EXPERIENCE ACROSS EXCHANGE SERVER AND EXCHANGE ONLINE

Whether your users are in the cloud or on-premises, they can all have the same experience of both the look and feel of your Exchange environment. All you will need to do is choosing a hybrid deployment and features such as free or busy status and calendar sharing will be available to all your users across the Exchange Server and Exchange Online.

To get further information about the hybrid deployments, visit Exchange Server 2013 hybrid deployments.

SAFEGUARDING YOUR EMAIL WITH EXCHANGE ONLINE PROTECTION

The configuration of Microsoft Exchange Online Protection gives you the liberty to safeguard your organization against spam and malware. It has features that enable you to guard your organization against violations of the messaging Policy. Ensure you study the best practices and properly configure Exchange Online Protection.

Visit Best practices for configuring Online Protection, for further information on Exchange Online protection.

HOW TO IMPROVE AND CUSTOMIZE YOUR SHAREPOINT ONLINE SITES

There are several ways to improve and customize SharePoint Online to enable you and your users to maximize your experience and become even more productive. You can explore and do the set up by following these simple steps:

- ❖ **Mailbox Site:** Activate the site mailboxes to store and organize projects or team-level email.
- ❖ **Configure Search Center:** the configuration of the Search Center allows you to be able to optimize users' search experience across sites.
- ❖ **Adding Apps to SharePoint:** adding the apps that you want to use on SharePoint sites enables you to provide targeted solutions for your end–users business needs. This can also be done by configuring the Business Connectivity Service (BSC)

which allows you to integrate the data that you stored in an external application.

Visit Manage site collections and global settings in the SharePoint Admin Center, for further information.

HOW TO EXTEND YOUR ON-PREMISES SHAREPOINT INVESTMENTS TO THE CLOUD

Microsoft Office 365 can be integrated with your SharePoint On-premises, and one of the most effective approaches you can use to efficiently integrate it to the cloud if you already have a functional SharePoint On-premises is hybrid deployment. This will enable you to do three things:

> ➢ To carry out a cross-premises search
> ➢ Application integration through Business Connectivity Services
> ➢ Integration of SAP processes using Duet Enterprise Online for Microsoft SharePoint.

Go to Hybrid SharePoint Server 13 for further information on how to extend your On-premises SharePoint investment to the cloud.

CHAPTER FOUR
THE EXPLOSION OF OFFICE 365 AND WHY

More than 1.2 billion people use Microsoft Office. Outlook.com has more than 400 million active users. Office 365 is now available in 140 markets in 40 languages. These are the latest official stats from Microsoft as of this writing. A much more interesting statistic, however, comes from Okta, a cloud service provider established in 2012, which offers passwords and employee accounts management for other cloud services. According to Okta, Office 365 has skyrocketed in a short span of 6 to 9 months, surpassing Salesforce as the most popular app used by their clients. As a consultant and a Microsoft Partner focused on helping small businesses with their cloud journey, it's easy for me to see why Office 365 is so popular. The latest iteration of Office 365 is the most secure cloud productivity and communications solution I've seen so far. It now includes such capabilities as;

- ★ Broadcasting web conferences to up to 10,000 people
- ★ Using Skype for Business like a traditional phone to make and receive phone calls to people outside your organization
- ★ Understanding work time and interactions
- ★ Ensuring that email attachments and links first pass through a "detonation" chamber for extra protection

When this book first came out, much of the productivity focus in Office 365 was on these services:

- ★ Email and calendar (Exchange Online)
- ★ Document collaboration (SharePoint Online)
- ★ Web conferencing (Lync Online—now called Skype for Business)
- ★ Office applications

Today, the Office 365 productivity story includes

- ★ Social networking (Yammer)
- ★ Professional digital storytelling (Sway)
- ★ Corporate YouTube portal (Office 365 Videos)
- ★ Personally relevant content for you (Office Delve)

The Different Microsoft Office 365 Plans

Office 365 is the answer to a modern workplace where people no longer have to work in the same location to get things done. As a cloud productivity and communication solution in one place, Microsoft Office 365 offers service plans for practically all types of businesses and organizations.

Analyzing the Of ice 365 Small Business Plans. For the price of one venti Caramel Macchiato (plus tax) from Starbucks, a small business can use 50-gigabyte mailbox 1 terabyte of online file storage (which is about $80 if you buy the same storage in a hard drive)

1. High-definition video conferencing
2. The online version of Microsoft Office
3. Social communication with colleagues

In other words, if you're a small business just starting out or a professional services provider working from home, there is no excuse for not impressing your customers or clients by exuding the perception of a large organization. All you have to do is give up one cup of coffee a month to be able to afford to subscribe to the Of ice 365 Business Essentials at $5 per user per month with an annual commitment.

If you already have a cloud-based email, subscribing to the Of ice 365 for Business plan gives you the newest version of Office for Mac and PC, Office apps you can run on your tablets and phones, online versions of Office including Word, Excel, and PowerPoint, 1 terabyte of online storage, and professional digital storytelling tools. This will cost you $8.25 per user per month with an annual commitment.

The Of ice 365 Business Premium plan, on the other hand, combines all the features of the two plans above into one integrated subscription for $12.50 per user month with an annual commitment.

All of the preceding plans have a 300-user limit, but they include;

a) Guaranteed 99.9 percent uptime, financially backed service level agreement
b) IT-level web support and 24/7 phone support for critical issues
c) Active Directory integration to easily manage user credentials and permissions

Breaking Down The Office 365 Enterprise Plans

Four enterprise Office 365 plans are ranging from $8 per user per month to $35 per user per month. You can have a variety of enterprise subscription plans based on the needs of your users. There is no limit to the number of users on the enterprise plans.

The table below shows lists of the cost (per user, per month) for the subscription and the key features associated with each of these plans.

Office 365 Enterprise Plans Pricing Model

- ❖ Office 365 Enterprise (per user, per month) E1 ($8) Pro Plus ($12)
  E3 ($20) E5 ($35)
  - ❖ Fully installed Office applications on up to 5 PCs or Macs per user (Office Pro Plus) ✓ ✓ ✓
  - ❖ Office on tablets and phones for the fully installed Office experience on up to 5 tablets and 5 phones per user ✓ ✓ ✓
  - ❖ Online versions of Office, including Word, Excel, and PowerPoint ✓ ✓ ✓ ✓
  - ❖ File storage and sharing with 1 TB storage per user (OneDrive for Business) ✓ ✓ ✓ ✓
  - ❖ Business-class email, calendar, and contacts (Exchange Online ✓
  - ❖ 50 GB inbox per user unlimited inbox ✓
  - ❖ Unlimited online meetings, IM, and audio, HD video, and web conferencing (Skype for Business) ✓ ✓ ✓
  - ❖ Intranet site with customizable security settings (SharePoint Online) ✓ ✓ ✓
  - ❖ Corporate social network (Yammer) ✓ ✓ ✓
  - ❖ Professional digital, interactive storytelling tool (Sway) ✓ ✓ ✓ ✓
  - ❖ Personalized search and discovery across Office 365 (Delve) ✓ ✓ ✓
  - ❖ Corporate video portal (Videos) ✓ ✓ ✓
  - ❖ Meeting broadcast on the Internet to up to 10,000 people (Skype for Business) ✓ ✓ ✓

- ❖ Discover, analyze, and visualize data in Excel ✓ ✓ ✓
- ❖ IT management of your apps, reports of usage, and shared computer activation ✓ ✓ ✓
- ❖ Compliance Center tools to support eDiscovery (important for your lawyers in case of litigation) ✓ ✓ ✓
- ❖ Compliance and information protection (archiving and legal hold, rights management, data loss prevention, and encryption for email and files) ✓ ✓
- ❖ Advanced Security for your data ✓
- ❖ Analytics tools to illustrate your own and your team's productivity (Power BI and Delve Analytics) ✓
- ❖ PSTN conferencing to allow invitees to join Skype for Business meetings by dialing in from a telephone ✓
- ❖ Cloud PBX for cloud-based call management to make, receive, and transfer calls across a wide range of devices ✓

Addressing The Needs Of Other Types Of Organizations

Not all organizations are created equal. Therefore, Microsoft has created the following plans to meet the requirements of non-business organizations.

OFFICE 365 EDUCATIONS

This plan offers free collaboration tools for students and teachers to enable them to work and learn together using best-in-class cloud technologies.

This is a great way to expose students to technologies they will be using in the workplace.

To take advantage of the free subscription for students and teachers, you must be verified as an academic institution, which usually takes 3-7 days. The best thing about this is that Exchange Online for email and calendar for alumni is provided as a free service even after the student graduates.

OFFICE 365 U.S. GOVERNMENTS

The U.S. government has unique needs and requirements when it comes to cloud technologies.

Therefore, Microsoft has created a segmented cloud community specifically designed to ensure these types of organizations meet U.S. compliance and security standards. This plan still provides all the features and capabilities of Office 365 for business, but it's only available to qualified U.S. government organizations, including federal, state, local, and tribal governments. Learn more

OFFICE 365 NONPROFIT

Qualified nonprofit organizations are eligible to receive basic Office 365 services as a donation.

The Office 365 Nonprofit Business Essentials is a free plan for up to 300 users, while the Office 365 Nonprofit E1 is free with unlimited users.

If your organization needs the advanced features, you can subscribe to the Office 365 Nonprofit Business Premium for $2 per user per month, or the Office 365 Nonprofit E3 for $4.50 per user per month.

CHAPTER FIVE
DISCOVERING OFFICE 365 FEATURES AND BENEFITS

Moving to the Office 365 cloud comes with some key features and benefits. Namely, your
The organization gets to continue to use the software you have been using for years, but you now get to shift the burden onto Microsoft. In addition to shifting the burden to Microsoft, we cover some other key benefits that we describe in the following sections.

★ Generating greater productivity
Productivity is a great word that management-consultant types love to use. In the real world though, productivity can be summed up in a simple question: Can I do my job easier or not? Microsoft has invested heavily and spent a tremendous amount of time trying to make the user and administrator experiences of Office 365 as easy and simple as possible.

★ **THE IDEA IS THAT INCREASING SIMPLICITY YIELDS GREATER PRODUCTIVITY;** Whether it is an administrator setting up a new employee or a business analyst working with big data and writing game-changing reports in Word. When the technology gets out of the way and you can focus on your job, you would become more productive. Just as using a typewriter instead of a word processor. For instance, whoever thought copy and paste would be such a game-changer?

★ **ACCESSING FROM ANYWHERE**
Accessing your enterprise software over the Internet has some big advantages. For one, all you need is your computer—desktop, laptop, tablet, or phone—and an Internet connection or phone coverage. Because the software is running in a Microsoft data center, you simply connect to the Internet to access the software.

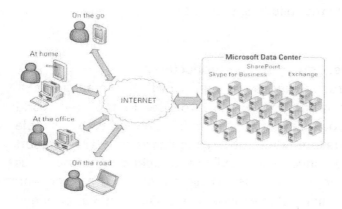

Accessing Office 365 software over the internet

Another advantage of accessing centrally located data is that you always have a single source of the truth. If you make a change to a document from your tablet at home and then your colleague views the file from her phone, she will see the most up-to-date document. Gone are the days of e-mailing Excel documents between machines with long file names, such as Forecast_D1_2019_KW Reviewed_donald-Edited-9-7-19_Revised_5-10-19_KW_final_More_edits_now-really FINAL.xlsx.
With SharePoint Online and OneDrive (part of the Office

365 package), a single file, say Forecast_D1_2019.xlsx lives out in the cloud (meaning in Microsoft's globally distributed billion-dollar data centers). Because the document lives in the cloud, the security permissions can be set up to allow anyone in the organization, regardless of geographic location, to view the document.

Security can be as strict or as lenient as desired. For instance, you may want everyone in the organization to be able to see a company policy document but only want a select group of individuals to edit the document. Also, SharePoint takes care of all of the versioning and even lets you check out a document to edit so that nobody else can edit it at the same time.

OneDrive for Business has taken on a life of its own, but it is still powered by SharePoint. Think of OneDrive for Business the same way you think of Dropbox or Box. It is personal cloud storage for your files. And remember that OneDrive is powered by SharePoint. In essence, OneDrive for Business is your personal file store, while a SharePoint library is shared across your organization.

Need to collaborate on the document in real-time? No problem. You can do that by using nothing more than your web browser as you find out in later chapters of the book. Working with what you know. Humans aren't very keen on change. We like to drive the same route to work for years before we figure out there is a better route that avoids all of those snarly traffic snafus.

Why would it be any different with the software you use daily?

Microsoft does not always come out with the best software. Remember Windows Vista and Windows 8? Shiver! Rather than running far away and never looking back at Windows again, users simply held their collective breath until Windows 7 and then Windows 10. And thank you for hurrying Microsoft! Microsoft Word, Excel, and PowerPoint have been in use for more than 20 years and even though new analysis software comes out all the time, Excel is still the one to beat. You know that you can do what you need to do without much headache.

One thing Microsoft did incredibly right recognizes that users don't want to give up the things that make them comfortable. "Don't take away our Word, Excel, and PowerPoint," we shouted!

And Microsoft listened. Office 365 hasn't changed our favorites one bit. The only difference is that now they are seamlessly connected to the enterprise software living out in the cloud. In other words, our favorite applications are cloudified.

One of the coolest features about SharePoint and Office is that you can work with SharePoint and One Drive without ever having to leave the Office applications. For example, you can fire up Word, check out a document stored in SharePoint or One Drive, make some changes, check it back in, review versions, and even leave some notes for your colleagues. All without even having to know SharePoint is handling the content management functionality behind the scenes.

❖ Robust security and reliability

With Microsoft taking on all of the responsibility for security and reliability, your IT team can rest on their laurels. After all, they spent their entire careers keeping the systems up and running. Shouldn't they get a break? All kidding aside, letting Microsoft do the heavy lifting frees up the IT team to do more important things. No, not playing computer games, but helping users get the most out of enterprise software. Ever wonder why nobody could ever find time to implement a company-wide blog and discussion board? Now they can finally be a reality. Microsoft understands if you aren't fully comfortable about letting them do the heavy lifting. In my opinion, it is the best scenario. After all, who better to handle managing software products than the same people who built them? To address some of the questions, however, Microsoft has an extensive service level agreement that helps in putting user's minds at ease.

❖ IT control and efficiency

If you have ever met an IT person, you might have generalized one thing about them. They are control freaks. They like to know exactly what everyone is doing with their systems at all times. If something goes wrong, then it is probably due to user error. Our systems do what they are supposed to do. Microsoft has gone out of its way to create an unprecedented level of control for administrators. But that is not all. Not only do administrators have control over the environment, but it is actually designed to be simple in nature and, get this, intuitive.

GETTING FAMILIAR WITH OFFICE 365 PRODUCTS

The Office 365 product is actually a package of products rented on a monthly basis. In particular, these include Office, SharePoint Online, OneDrive for Business, Exchange Online, and Skype for Business Online.
The online part just means that you access these server products over the Internet. If your IT team were to buy these products and install them for your use in the company data center, then they would be called on-premise.

- **Microsoft Office**

Finding someone who doesn't use some aspect of Microsoft Office on a daily basis is difficult. Whether it is Outlook for email, Word for creating and editing documents, Excel for manipulating data, and PowerPoint for creating and making presentations, these old standbys seem to dominate the life of the modern-day information worker.

The newest version of Office came out in 2016. When you have Office 365, you pay on a monthly basis and can always be assured you have the latest version of Office installed on your device.
Microsoft Office includes much more than these old stalwarts, though. In particular, Office includes the

following applications:

1) Word: Microsoft Office Word is used for word processing, such as creating and editing documents.
2) Excel: Excel is used for data analysis and numeric manipulation.
3) PowerPoint: PowerPoint is used to create and deliver presentations.
4) Outlook: An application that is used for email, contacts, and calendaring including scheduling meetings, meeting rooms, and other resources.
5) OneNote: An application that is used for capturing and organizing notes.
6) Publisher: An application that is used to create and share publications and marketing materials, such as brochures, newsletters, postcards, and greeting cards.
7) Access: A database application that is used to collect, store, manipulate, and report on data.
8) SharePoint: SharePoint is a web-based platform that lets you easily create an Intranet for your organization. An Intranet is just an internal-only website where you find content, see company policies, and find other such internal tasks.
9) OneDrive for Business: OneDrive for Business is a cloud-based, file storage service that is part of Office 365. If you're tech-savvy, you will quickly recognize that OneDrive for Business is powered by SharePoint.
10) Delve: Delve is a newcomer to Office 365. Think of it as an extension to SharePoint and OneDrive. Delve helps you handle the deluge of digital content. Delve shows you content it thinks you

want to see, and learns from your behaviors as you work. For example, you might see the latest content your immediate coworkers have updated or updates to content you have had an interest in previously.

11) Power BI: Power BI is not necessarily a part of the traditional Microsoft Office, but it falls squarely within the Office 365 suite of critical applications. Power BI was born in the cloud and has only ever lived in the cloud. Power BI is designed to take the mountains of data from all over the place and help you make sense of it through reports, dashboards, and other analysis tools.

12) Skype for Business: When you need to connect with other people, Skype is the tool for you Skype for Business allows you to connect with others using features such as instant messaging

13) and conferencing including screen sharing, polling, and shared presentations. Using Skype for Business, you can also add regular old Skype users to your business communications.

Pay-As-You-Go Flexibility

14) With pay-as-you-go licensing your organization is able to turn on or off licensing, depending on the number of users that require Office 365. In addition, Microsoft has added flexibility for you as a user by allowing you to activate the licensing on up to five different computers at a single time, depending on your plan. For example, when your organization adds you as an Office 365 subscriber, you can activate the software on your workstation

at work, your laptop, your home computer, and your home laptop. When you buy a new computer, you will find a simple user screen where you can update the computers that Office is activated on. This flexibility makes managing your Office applications and licensing as easy and straightforward as possible.

Native Apps Experience Integrated Into Web Apps

In addition to running Office applications, such as Word, Excel, PowerPoint, and Outlook on your local computer, Office 365 also includes a web version of these applications called Office Online Apps and mobile versions called Office Mobile. When working with the Office Online Apps, you simply open your web browser and browse to your SharePoint portal that contains your document. You can then open or edit your document right in the web browser. Likewise, when using the Mobile Apps you open up the mobile version of the Office app, such as Word, on your mobile device and edit it, just like you would on your laptop or desktop computer.

Microsoft has gone to great pains to make the Office Online Apps and Mobile Apps experience very similar to the traditional Office experience. For example, when you are checking email in Outlook, writing a Word document, or reviewing or editing an Excel document or PowerPoint presentation you expect certain behavior. Microsoft has tried very hard to retain the familiar feel of the Office you love.

Latest Versions Of The Office Apps—Always

Because Office 365 uses a SaaS model, you are always instantly up to date. When Microsoft releases a new version of Office, your licensing is instantly upgraded. You don't need to wait for the IT team to finally get the new product purchased and rolled out. When Microsoft flips the switch, everyone has the latest and greatest instantly available. Severing ties to Your Desk If you are used to using Outlook for your email, then you won't experience any changes when your organization moves to Office 365. The only difference will be that Microsoft is now hosting your email instead of your local IT department. Should you decide to look a bit further, however, you can find a great deal of extra functionality just waiting to make your life easier. For example, the new Outlook Mobile apps are integrated with Exchange in order to push email directly to your phone whether you use iPhone, Android, or a Windows phone. If you prefer a different email app, No problem. Almost every email app on the market can be setup to receive Office 365 email.

Using Outlook Online

Office 365 provides the ability for you to check your enterprise Exchange email using nothing more than a web browser. Instead of using Outlook on your local computer you simply browse to a web address, such as http://mail.myorganization.com, and then log in and check your email.
The experience is very similar to other web email services, such as;

    I.   Google's Gmail or
   II.   Microsoft's Hotmail.

What's exciting about Outlook Online, however, is that you finally get access to your enterprise email, calendar, and contacts from any computer with an Internet connection and a web browser.

Outlook and Exchange are both email-related products, but one is for users and the other is server software. Exchange is a server product that sits on a server in a data center and manages all of your emails. The outlook is an application that you install on your local desktop and then use to connect to the Exchange server to check and manage your email, contacts, and calendaring. With Office 365, you still use Outlook (installed on your local computer or phone) but instead of connecting to an Exchange server managed by your IT team, you connect to an Exchange server managed by Microsoft.

Grouping Conversations In Your Inbox

Like it or not, email has become a primary means of communication for the modern information worker. It is not uncommon for many people to send and receive a truck load of emails on a daily, if not hourly, basis. Keeping track of different emails on different topics with different people can be a daunting task. Outlook 2016 has a feature geared towards helping you keep track of all of those conversations. The feature automatically groups conversations by subject, as shown in the figure below.

Show as Conversations checkbox

Proposal conversation

Notice that the Proposal is the subject of the emails and the entire conversation is grouped for easy reading. You can even see your response emails and any meetings associated with this conversation. No more digging through your Sent box looking for how you responded to a particular email. You can turn on the Conversations feature by clicking on the View tab in Outlook and then checking the Show as Conversations checkbox, as shown in the image above.

Getting Organized With Of Ice 365 Groups

Office 365 is constantly adding features, and a relatively new one is called Office 365 Groups. The Groups feature is aptly named, because it allows you to create public and private groups. Outlook 2016 is one component of Office that takes advantage of Office 365 Groups. Other apps that work with Office 365 Groups include;

    i.   OneDrive for Business

ii.   for Business, and
iii.   OneNote.

Microsoft has plans to integrate most of the Office 365 apps with Groups, so if you have a favorite, check whether Groups is already available.

When a new member joins a group, they can see the history of the group and quickly get up to speed. Everyone in the group can;

- ❖ chat with each other
- ❖ Share files
- ❖ schedule meetings
- ❖ Share notes, and
- ❖ Use Skype for Business for real-time communication.

You Can Now Have Your Own Personal Archiving Experience

Exchange Online gives you access to your own personal email archiving system. Your personal archive shows up as another mailbox right next to your regular mailbox. You access your archive just like you access your regular mailbox. On top of that, when you need to search for an old email, you can choose to search your archive in addition to your regular mailbox.

Create Unique Communities For Your Organization And Corporate World

An online community is nothing more than a group of people coming together by using their computers regardless of geographic location. If you have used Facebook or LinkedIn or even AOL or Yahoo Groups, then you have been involved in an online community. SharePoint brings online communities to the corporate world in a secure corporate environment. You can imagine the scenario where you are in the accounting department and the team is working on company financials. The team needs to collaborate with each other, but you wouldn't want to be posting to each other's Facebook walls or Twitter accounts. Some of the online community features that SharePoint provides include;

Wiki's, blogs, content tagging, document sharing, discussion boards, people search, alerts, and notifications.

In addition to the online community features already discussed, every person who has a SharePoint account also has his or her own personal online file store that is powered by SharePoint. This feature is called OneDrive for Business; it allows you to store your files and share them with others. If you are familiar with Dropbox, Box, or Google Drive, then you already understand the concept of cloud-based file storage. OneDrive for Business comes with most Office 365 subscriptions, so you don't have to go searching for it. You access it on the Office 365 waffle, along with the rest of your Office 365 apps. The Office 365 waffle is shown below.

Accessing office 365 using the "waffle

Depending on the resolution of your screen, the waffle will show up in the upper left or the upper right of your browser screen.

VBC Library
289 Factory RD
Clinton, AR 72031
501-745-2100 www.fcl.org

700455

SHARING INFORMATION WITH CUSTOMERS AND PARTNERS WITH EXTRANET SITES

Because SharePoint Online (one of the components of Office 365) is online, you have the ability to share information with partners that are not part of your local network. These sites that you can make available to people outside your organization are called extranet sites. An example of an extranet site might be a partner network made up of complementary companies. The people in these other companies won't have access to your company network, but you still need to be able to share information and collaborate with them. SharePoint Online offers extranet sites for just such a purpose.

Microsoft has gone to great lengths to create a secure, safe, and stable SharePoint environment. In particular, Microsoft guarantees the following:

The environment is available 99.9 percent of the time

All content and configuration details are backed up regularly

Virus scanning software for SharePoint constantly scans content for threats

File types that can pose a risk to your SharePoint environment are blocked from upload

Microsoft Office 365 is truly a global product with data center locations distributed throughout the world. The product supports more than 40 languages including Chinese, Arabic, Spanish, and Portuguese. Need your site to support the Catalan language? No problem, SharePoint Online has you covered.

Going Virtual with Intuitive Communications

Skype for Business Online is the latest iteration of Microsoft's cloud-based communications service. In particular, you can chat through text, talk to people using voice, and even have face-to-face meetings by using your webcam. In addition, Skype for Business allows you to conduct online meetings by using screen sharing, virtual whiteboards, electronic file sharing, and even online polling.

Text/Voice/Video in a single app and service

You can think of the Skype for Business application as a one-stop-shop for instant communication. Because Microsoft has tightly integrated the Office 365 applications, you can move seamlessly between them. For example, you might be reading a post on SharePoint and want to instantly communicate with the poster. You can view the presence icon and if it is green that means the user is available. Or maybe you are reading your email and want to see whether the person that sent you the email is available for a chat. From within the Outlook Online App, you can see the Skype for the Business status of the user. If it is green, then the person is available and you can instantly open Skype for Business and communicate. The Skype for Business status shown in Outlook Online App is shown in the figure below.

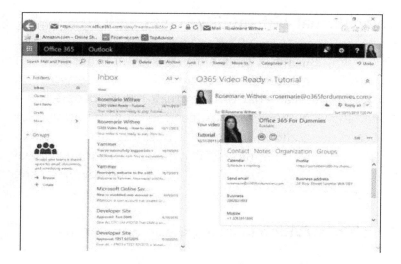

Instantly communicating with users using Skype for Business from within the Outlook Online App

As you are chatting with the person that posted, you might decide that you want to share screens and invite others to join the meeting. By using Skype for Business, it is as simple as a couple of button clicks.

From Conversations To Ad Hoc Meetings—Yes, It's Possible

By using Skype for Business, you can instantly connect with others from multiple locations. As previously mentioned, you might be reading a SharePoint post but you also might receive an email and want to meet with that person right away if he is available. You can see his status on the presence icon next to his name in your Outlook email message. If you want to communicate with this person, you can hover over his Skype for Business presence icon to access the Skype for Business menu. You may want to send a chat message to the user, so you click the Chat button. A chat session will instantly open, and Skype for Business takes care of pulling in the subject of the email as the subject of the chat so that the person knows what the chat is about. It's almost as good as walking across the hall to talk to someone, only now that someone can be anywhere in the world.

Online Meetings Unleashed

An online meeting is nothing new. There are many services that offer the ability to share your screen or co-author documents. What has finally come together with Office 365 is the tight integration between all of the different products. You can now see if someone is available for a meeting right from within the applications you use day in and day out, such as;

i.   Outlook,
ii.   Office, and
iii. SharePoint.

Using Skype for Business;- it is also possible to set up meetings with those outside your organization. Skype for Business meetings enable you to conduct meetings using chat rooms, audio, video, shared whiteboards, and even polling, etc.

Interacting With Photos And Activity Feeds

In addition to instant communication, Skype for Business can also contain personal information, such as photos and activity feeds. Being able to put a face with a name is nice. Just about anywhere you might connect with another person, be it Outlook, SharePoint, or the author information property from within an Office document, you can view information about the person. The name of a person will have a presence icon next to it. Hover over the presence icon or photo and then click the details screen. The figure below illustrates viewing the details of a colleague from within the Author property of a Word document.

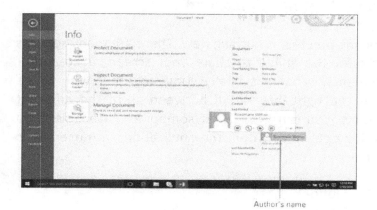

Author's name

Viewing information about who authored a particular word document

The activity feed is a current status sentence similar to Twitter but on a corporate level. For example, you might be headed down working on a document and update your status with "Working heads down on a document but here if you need me in a pinch!" Other users will see this status message and know that even though you are online at the moment you are busy working on a document. Of course, another use for the status message could be something along the lines of, "Leftover cake in the break room! Get it while it lasts!"

CONCLUSION

Office 365 is the game–changer of the 21st century for small, medium, and large scale businesses, organizations (big and small) as well as internet savvy IT professionals. It has changed the narrative for personal businesses and organizations alike as it allows Organizations large and small to move their infrastructure over to the cloud to reap the cost savings, predictability, and peace of mind that comes with the cloud operations.

Office 365 is the cloud–based subscription model version of Microsoft's popular productivity suit–Microsoft Office.

Microsoft has included most of their popular Enterprise products in Office 365, thus, have eased the complexity of keeping the software running in the business equation.

Office 365 can be classified under two broad categories: the first covers consumers (personal businesses or individuals who directly utilizes the services on Office 365 to store data or access stored data, host or connect to cloud meetings from their devices such as mobile phones, laptop computers, etc, and the second covers corporate, non–profits organizations, governments, schools as well as other large organizations.

You have learned how to all the steps you would take to register or sign up for and start using Office 365 effectively, whether for yourself or your organization and how you can comfortably add users and collaborate.

No more limitation: You can run now set and run your businesses Online; connect your colleagues, partners, and associates from the comfort of your home, or anywhere in the world as long as you have an internet device.

CPSIA information can be obtained
at www.ICGtesting.com
Printed in the USA
LVHW080954101021
700051LV00021B/424